Y0-DRX-370

100%

Children's Room
133 Elm Street
New Haven, Conn. 06510

SEP 2 4 1992

SEP 2 4 2016

DATE DUE

OCT 2 2 1992   MAY 2 3 2015

NOV 2 9 1993   SEP 2 4 2014

NOV 1 - 1994

AUG 2 3 1996

AUG 1 1 1998

FEB 1 2 2000

AUG 2 8 2003

DEC 0 5 2009

JUN 0 2 2012

JUN 0 8 2013

SEP 1 1 2013

MAY 1 9 2014

THE RACE TO THE
SOUTH POLE

Rupert Matthews

Illustrated by Doug Post

The Bookwright Press
New York · 1989

Great Journeys

The First Men on the Moon
The Travels of Marco Polo
The Voyage of the Beagle
The Race to the South Pole

Further titles are in
preparation

Cover Captain Scott
leads his party toward
the South Pole.

Frontispiece The
rugged, barren
landscape of Antarctica.

First published in the
United States in 1989 by
The Bookwright Press
387 Park Avenue South
New York, NY 10016

First published in 1989 by
Wayland (Publishers) Limited
61 Western Road, Hove
East Sussex BN3 1JD, England

© Copyright 1989 Wayland (Publishers)
Limited

Typeset by DP Press Ltd, Sevenoaks, Kent
Printed in Italy by G. Canale & C.S.p.A.,
Turin

Library of Congress Cataloging-in-
Publication Data
Matthews, Rupert
 The race to the South Pole / by Rupert
Matthews.
  p. cm.—(Great journeys)
 Bibliography: p.
 Includes index.
 Summary: An account of the
competition between explorers to reach
the South Pole with emphasis on the
events of the rival expeditions led by the
Norwegian Roald Amundsen and the
British Robert Scott between 1910 and
1913.
 ISBN 0–531–18273–8
 1. Scott, Robert Falcon, 1868–1912—
Journeys—Juvenile literature. 2.
Amundsen, Roald, 1872–1928—
Journeys—Juvenile literature. 3. British
Antarctic ("Terra Nova") Expedition,
1910–1913—Juvenile literature. 4. South
Pole—Juvenile literature. [1. British
Antarctic ("Terra Nova") Expedition,
1910–1913. 2. Scott, Robert Falcon, 1868–
1912. 3. Amundsen, Roald, 1872–1928. 4.
South Pole.]
I. Title.   II. Series.
G850 1910.S4M37 1989
919.8′904–dc19   88–7534
                                    CIP
                                    AC

Contents

The Edge of the Unknown

Until the eighteenth century nobody knew much about Antarctica. Not one explorer had traveled within 2,000 km (1,250 mi) of the South Pole. It was a massive and completely unexplored part of the world.

The lack of information about this area did not stop European scientists from making guesses about the land surrounding the Pole. Map makers drew what they thought was there and geographers invented theories to hide their lack of knowledge. One of the most common ideas in the eighteenth century was that there was a huge continent at the South Pole. On maps of the time, this enormous land stretches as far as 40 degrees south. Whenever islands were sighted in this area they were presumed to be part of this giant continent.

In 1768 Captain James Cook left the port of Plymouth in Britain, with orders to sail to Tahiti and set up an observatory there. The second part of his journey had been kept secret until he had sailed; he was ordered to travel 50 degrees south to find if a "land of great extent" actually lay where the scientists had predicted. He found nothing. On later voyages, Cook sailed even farther south, reaching 71 degrees. Still no land was sighted. Cook turned north, certain that there was no land around the South Pole.

Right Captain James Cook, probably the first European to sail into Antarctic waters.

Below A map showing the position of Antarctica, which includes the South Pole and the surrounding area.

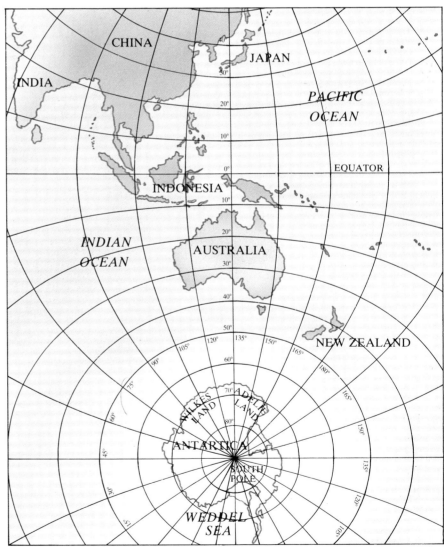

Seventy years later, in 1839, three more expeditions set out to find the Antarctic continent and prove that Cook was wrong. An American team led by Lieutenant Charles Wilkes sailed south through stormy, iceberg-filled seas until at long last, land was sighted. This section of Antarctica is now called Wilkes Land. Due to bad planning, Wilkes had to turn back early, and he was still uncertain whether he had found an island or a continent.

A French team, under Jules Dumont d'Urville, sighted Antarctica just one day after Wilkes. D'Urville sailed east along a section of the coast of Antarctica, now called Adelie Land. It soon became clear that even if Antarctica was not a continent it was a huge island.

The most important expedition of 1839 was led by James Clark Ross of the British Royal Navy. With two ships under his command, Ross reached Antarctica in January 1841. He had better ships and equipment than the other expeditions and was therefore able to remain in the southern oceans until 1843. He charted hundreds of miles of coastline, including Victoria Land and the Ross Ice Shelf, which was named after him.

The Ross Ice Shelf is a magnificent natural wonder. From the sea it appears to be a solid wall of ice over 650 km (400 mi) long and about 60 m (200 ft) tall. Massive icebergs, some the size of Connecticut, break off and drift northward.

Left Sir James Clark Ross who spent two years exploring the coasts of Antarctica. He discovered the Ross Ice Shelf, which was later named in his honor.

Their loss is replaced by fresh snow, which falls on the Ice Shelf and the land beyond it. The Ice Shelf floats on the surface of the Antarctic Ocean. It covers an area roughly the size of France, and is one of the most incredible natural formations in the world.

Above The spectacular ice cliffs that form the seaward edge of the Ross Ice Shelf.

The Antarctic Year

After the expeditions of Wilkes, Ross and d'Urville, little effort was made to explore Antarctica. Then, in 1894, an Australian expedition became one of the first groups to land there. In 1899 the first expedition to winter in Antarctica set out from England.

An international gathering of geographers was held in Germany the following year. This event, which was called the Berlin Geographical Congress, included discussions of many aspects of map-making and exploration. The geographers decided that Antarctica was the most important unexplored region in the world, and an International Antarctica Year was announced. Scientists all over the world were then encouraged to study the southern polar regions.

In 1901 two expeditions set out to try to land on Antarctica and gather information. The first, which was led by Nils Otto Nordenskjöld, came from Sweden. This team landed on Graham Land and explored large areas of the peninsula, which points toward South America.

The second team was British. Their expedition had been planned several years earlier. Sir Clements Markham had gained the support of both the Royal Society and the Royal Geographical Society for this expedition. The team was to

Above *The base camp of the* **British** Discovery *Expedition of 1901–04.*

conduct scientific experiments, collect information about the climate and explore as much of the land as they could. The two societies chose a young naval commander named Robert Falcon Scott to lead the team.

In the months leading up to the team's departure, Scott found out as much as he could about Polar conditions. He became friends with Fridtjof Nansen, a Norwegian explorer who had traveled widely in the Arctic Ocean. Such experienced men as Nansen helped Scott to choose equipment and stores for the voyage. The expedition took enough supplies to last for many months. To keep the team

Above *A portrait of Captain Scott in his naval uniform.*

Right *Scott and his team used dogs in the 1901–04 expedition, but found that they were unreliable for heavy work.*

Above *Nils Otto Nordenskjöld.*

Below *Fridtjof Nansen.*

happy, luxuries such as roast pheasants, rump steak and champagne were taken to be used on special occasions. Scott's ship, the *Discovery*, was specially built for the voyage.

The *Discovery*, with her crew of 47 sailors and scientists, arrived off Antarctica at the height of the southern summer, in January 1902. They landed on Ross Island, at the western edge of the Ross Ice Shelf. They unloaded the ship and built a hut strong enough to withstand the winter weather. (In fact, the men spent most of their time in Antarctica on the ship.)

Winter, with its continuous darkness, began around the end of April. The temperature fell to a low of –40°C (–40°F). The men had to keep quite close to the ship because of the freezing cold. They spent their time collecting wildlife specimens and carrying out various experiments. When the summer came, exploration became possible again and replaced these activities.

Of the several teams that set out, the most important was led by Scott, who was accompanied by Edward Wilson and Ernest Shackleton. The team, which had five sleds, drawn by dogs, moved south across the Ross Ice Shelf, hoping to discover how large it was and what lay beyond it. After two months, they had covered over 600 km (375 mi) and had reached the other side of the Ice Shelf. They discovered vast mountain ranges, and Mount Markham, Antarctica's highest peak at 4,600 m (15,100 ft). On the return trip all the dogs died from cold and overwork, and the explorers had to drag the sleds themselves. After a long struggle, they reached the ship. Other parties had gone west into Victoria Land and across Ross Island. When the expedition left Antarctica in 1903 they had added greatly to the knowledge of this great continent.

Shackleton's Attempt

In 1904, after its return journey, the British Antarctic team split up. The scientists began writing up their notes and working out the results of their experiments. The naval officers returned to sea. However, Scott was allowed a few months leave to write a book and give talks about the expedition. Within a few years it looked as if they had all settled back into ordinary life. But this was not to be.

Following the voyage of the *Discovery*, several other expeditions also traveled to Antarctica. The most successful of these included German and French groups, which explored inland areas and long sections of coastline. Many people in

Britain began to fear that because of the hard work carried out by the British Antarctic Expedition other countries would get to the South Pole first. They tried to persuade Scott to lead another team south, and tried to get financial backing from the British government for the trip.

Suddenly, in February 1907, Shackleton surprised everyone by announcing that he was to lead a scientific expedition to Antarctica and would do his best to reach the South Pole. Even more amazing to Scott and other

Left Ernest Shackleton.

Below Shackleton's sleds were pulled by Siberian ponies, which were both strong and reliable.

explorers was the fact that Shackleton already had plenty of money. He had collected funds from several rich businessmen who were interested in polar exploration. In order not to anger Scott and scientific institutions by taking advantage of the work of the earlier expedition, Shackleton agreed not to use Scott's old base but to find his own.

When Shackleton arrived in Antarctica in January 1908, he explored long stretches of the coastline, but could not find a suitable spot to anchor his ship. With winter approaching he headed for Ross Island and camped not far from the 1902 base. When Scott learned of this broken promise he was furious. He never forgave Shackleton.

Meanwhile, Shackleton prepared for the winter. As in Scott's earlier expedition, Shackleton's team spent the dark winter months carrying out scientific experiments, which were as important and complicated as any that had been undertaken at that time.

When spring arrived, Shackleton prepared for his journey to the South Pole. Disappointed with the dogs that had been used in 1902, Shackleton had taken only a few with him. Instead he relied on tough Siberian ponies. One of his most imaginative ideas was the use of an Arrol Johnston motor car that he had brought with him. The ponies and the car worked well for a time, but the car became stuck in soft snow, and eventually the ponies died.

Shackleton almost managed to reach the South Pole. He crossed the Ross Ice Shelf and found a route through the mountains surrounding it. This route took him along a huge glacier that sloped gently upward. Shackleton called it the Beardmore Glacier after one of the men who had given him the money for the journey. Beyond the glacier, Shackleton and his three companions found a plateau that stretched out of sight to the south. For several days the men hurried south, but bad weather soon slowed them down. On January 9, 1909 lack of food forced Shackleton to turn back. He was only 160 km (100 mi) from the South Pole.

Raising Funds

When Shackleton returned home in March 1909, the whole world waited for his news. The expedition's scientific work was quickly taken up by scholars. However, most people were disappointed that the team had not reached the South Pole. When Scott heard that the Pole had not yet been conquered he said, "I think we'd better have a shot next."

Other events influenced Scott in his decision to travel south. Many scientists were criticizing the work that had been undertaken during Scott's first expedition. They said the research work had not been accurate enough, but did not think about the extremely low temperatures and terrible blizzards in which the work had been carried out. Scott wanted to show that he and his men were capable of excellent scientific experiments.

Scott announced his plans in the summer of 1909. He said that he would lead a huge scientific expedition to Antarctica and intended to reach the South Pole. Such a journey had to be paid for and Scott's plans would cost an enormous amount. Scott and his supporters began the task of raising funds.

This was far from easy. The government refused to give them any money, but they did agree to allow naval officers to

Captain Scott.

A.C. Cherry-Garrard.

Lieutenant Bowers.

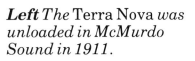

Left *The* Terra Nova *was unloaded in McMurdo Sound in 1911.*

Left *Setting up base camp in January 1911. Unlike the earlier expedition, the men lived on shore for much of the time.*

take leave in order to be part of the team. Scott set out on a wide tour of Britain, giving talks about polar exploration and the benefits to be gained by the new expedition. Money was collected at these meetings and local groups were also asked to help. Sometimes they only collected a small amount, but on other occasions they had better luck. The money was beginning to arrive and some equipment could now be bought.

The most expensive item needed was a ship. After looking at several vessels, Scott decided on the *Terra Nova*, which was strong and had plenty of room. It cost a great deal of money, but by this time enough funds had been raised. Huntley and Palmers, an English biscuit maker, baked large amounts of special biscuits that were suited to Antarctic conditions. Other special food was bought to help the explorers stay healthy in sub-zero temperatures. Scott asked the advice of his old friend, Fridtjof Nansen, about the clothing and transportation that would be needed.

The team was also being chosen. Many members of the earlier 1901 expedition wanted to join and were accepted by Scott. Edward Wilson was taken on as chief scientist and put in charge of selecting a group of scientists to work with him, but Scott chose the rest of the team himself. By the summer of 1910 the expedition was ready to set out. The team was chosen very carefully. Henry "Birdie" Bowers was a serving marine, Apsley Cherry-Garrard contributed to the expedition funds and worked without pay, Herbert Ponting was a well-known photographer, and Captain Lawrence Oates had great experience of animals.

Captain "Titus" Oates.

Herbert Ponting.

Petty Officer Evans.

Scott Sails

The *Terra Nova* sailed from London on June 1, 1910. The ship was packed with the very latest equipment. The scientific team was highly qualified and included two naturalists, three geologists and meteorologists.

On the long voyage the men did not waste their time but carried out many experiments and investigations. On the island of South Trinidad, for example, the team discovered ten different sorts of spiders that were previously unknown. Wilson and Cherry-Garrard spent time catching and studying sea birds. When they were not working, the men spent their time getting to know each other and playing games.

The *Terra Nova* stopped at several ports on its way to Ross Island. At Cape Town, Melbourne and Wellington the ship was welcomed and parties were given for the crew. After a stop at Port Chalmers the *Terra Nova* turned for Antarctica. On January 4, 1911 they arrived in McMurdo Sound and the team established a base camp at Cape Evans.

Scott had brought along a ready-made hut, which measured 18 m by 9 m (59 ft × 30 ft). The team would live in this hut during their stay.

The route taken by the Terra Nova *on its voyage from London to McMurdo Sound. The scientists on board carried out experiments during the journey.*

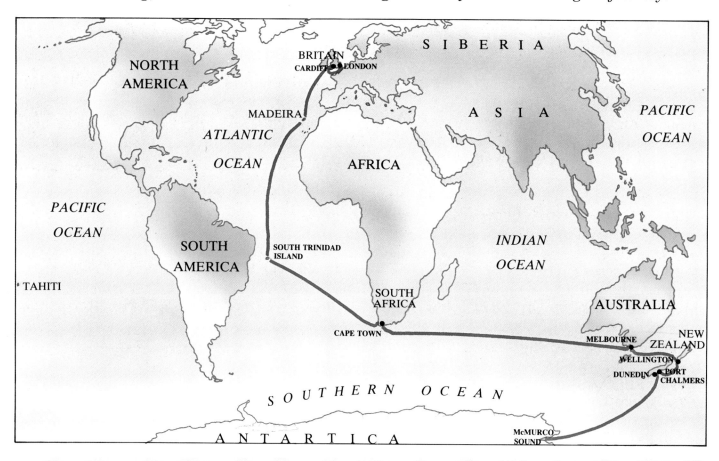

Left One of the motorized sleds and its crew in October 1911. From left to right the men are Lieutenant Evans, Day, Lashly and Hooper.

The scientific equipment was unloaded and set up so that work could begin as soon as possible. The scientists began their work immediately. The naturalists studied penguins and seals and tried to capture as many fish as possible. The team's meteorologists took daily weather readings. Everyone was busy.

Transportation was perhaps the most important problem faced by the team. Scott organized his journeys much the way Shackleton had in 1908. He had brought with him dogs, ponies and motorized sleds. Scott did not think that dogs were useful on long journeys. His experience in 1902 had shown that dogs could move fast when pulling only a small amount, but did not like dragging fully loaded sleds. The three tractor-like sleds he had brought were better suited to Arctic conditions than Shackleton's car had been, as they had tracks similar to those of a tank instead of tires.

Scott had brought the tractors so he could test them in Antarctic conditions and suggest improvements to their makers. Unfortunately, one of the machines fell through the ice soon after it was unloaded. It was the Siberian ponies that Scott relied on to help the men. These animals were able to withstand very low temperatures and could pull a heavier weight than either men or dogs.

Above Conditions in the hut were cramped. The men had to sleep amid a jumble of equipment and clothing.

Amundsen Turns South

When he had stopped at Melbourne, Scott had received a telegram that shocked the whole team. It read simply "Beg leave inform you proceeding Antarctic, Amundsen." When the news became known, the Norwegian Roald Amundsen was not at all popular. Newspaper articles criticized Amundsen for making his arrangements secretly. Bowers, one of Scott's team, wrote, "I regard him as a backhanded sneaking ruffian."

Amundsen's telegram caused bad feeling because of what had happened earlier. For many months the scientific world had known that Scott would be leading an expedition to Antarctica, hoping to reach the South Pole. He had announced his plans to other polar explorers and they had informed him of theirs. By informing each other in this way, different teams were able to help each other and would not carry out identical work.

Amundsen seemed to be following these unwritten rules. He announced that he was sailing north in order "to study in a scientific manner the polar sea." In this way he managed to collect money from various men who were interested in science and the Arctic. He even borrowed his ship, the *Fram*, from Scott's old friend Nansen. Amundsen was tricking everyone, even his own crew.

He was determined to reach the South Pole before Scott. He wrote, "If I was to maintain my prestige as an explorer, I must quickly achieve a success." It was his secrecy that shocked the British team. If Amundsen's sponsors had known of his true intentions they would probably

Right *Roald Amundsen in his special Antarctic clothing, based upon traditional Inuit (Eskimo) designs.*

Below *Amundsen used highly trained dogs to pull his sleds.*

not have given him their money, and Nansen would not have lent him his ship.

Amundsen had made his plans well. Until Scott received his telegram only Amundsen's brother and the captain of the *Fram* had known they would be heading south. He had left the telegram in a sealed envelope, with instructions that it was not to be sent until after the *Fram* had left port.

Amundsen had taken no radio on the *Fram* so nobody could get in touch with him after he had set out. He was determined not to be called back by Nansen or anybody else.

Unlike Scott, Amundsen did not intend to carry out any scientific investigations on the journey. He was going to rush to the South Pole and back again. Because he wanted to move fast and did not have to carry much, he took equipment quite different from Scott's. While Scott was relying on motorized sleds and ponies to drag the team's heavy equipment, Amundsen needed only dogs. The dog teams, carrying light loads, could dash at high speed across the snow. He bought the best dogs he could find and trained them in the best methods of sleding. Amundsen was determined to work his dogs as hard as he could. He pushed them to the limits of their strength, and when an exhausted dog dropped dead, Amundsen had it cut up and fed to the others. In this way he would be able to reach the South Pole and return to the coast quickly, but he would be left with no means of transportation for any further attempts.

Amundsen's Gamble

During the short weeks of the Antarctic autumn, Scott organized his team. Sleding parties set out to store food and other supplies at various points on the Ice Shelf. These supplies were to be used in the spring by exploration parties, and they would cut down the amount that would need to be carried on the sleds. On one of these trips eight of the nineteen ponies were carried out to sea when the ice on which they were standing broke up and drifted away. They were then attacked by killer whales and only two of them survived.

A party led by Victor Campbell set out in the *Terra Nova* to explore King Edward VII Land, on the other side of the Ice Shelf. On their way back, they came across the *Fram*, anchored in the Bay of Whales. This shallow bay in the Ross Ice Shelf had been chosen by Amundsen for two reasons. It was the only stable part of the Shelf and it was the closest point to the South Pole that could be reached by sea. The two groups met but they were both careful not to give away too many of their plans to each other.

The crew of the *Terra Nova* hurried back to tell Scott about the *Fram*, and then sailed on to New Zealand. It had been planned that the ship would collect supplies there and return to Antarctica in the spring. A group led by Campbell was

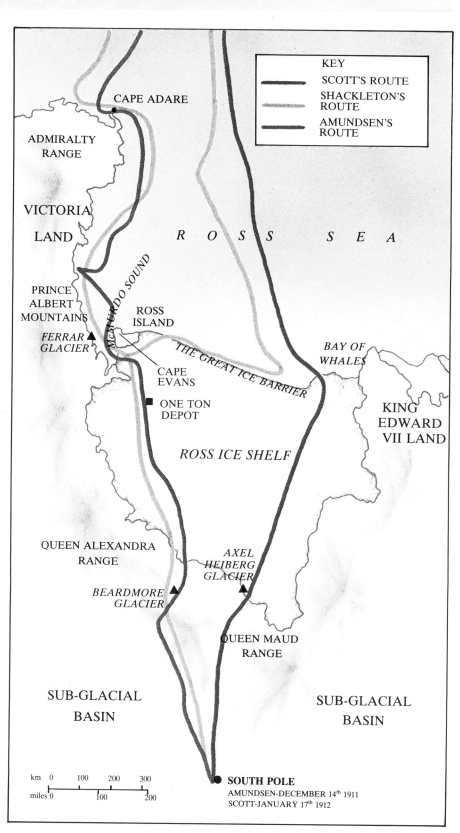

KEY
SCOTT'S ROUTE
SHACKLETON'S ROUTE
AMUNDSEN'S ROUTE

CAPE ADARE

ADMIRALTY RANGE

VICTORIA LAND

R O S S   S E A

PRINCE ALBERT MOUNTAINS

FERRAR GLACIER

McMURDO SOUND

ROSS ISLAND

CAPE EVANS

THE GREAT ICE BARRIER

BAY OF WHALES

ONE TON DEPOT

ROSS ICE SHELF

KING EDWARD VII LAND

QUEEN ALEXANDRA RANGE

AXEL HEIBERG GLACIER

BEARDMORE GLACIER

QUEEN MAUD RANGE

SUB-GLACIAL BASIN

SUB-GLACIAL BASIN

km 0   100   200   300
miles 0   100   200

SOUTH POLE
AMUNDSEN-DECEMBER 14th 1911
SCOTT-JANUARY 17th 1912

dropped off on Victoria Land, where they carried out much valuable work.

The long, cold winter began. The British team settled down to some serious scientific work. Wilson, together with Cherry-Garrard and Bowers, set out on a nightmare journey across the Ice Shelf to reach a colony of emperor penguins. Traveling in darkness, relieved only by moonlight, they marched the 110 km (68 mi) in terrible conditions. "I was beginning to think I could stand anything," wrote Bowers, "but when one has to deal with 109 degrees below freezing point [−77° C] I did not want to ask for more." They collected the penguin eggs they wanted and then returned to their camp safely.

Scott divided his time between scientific experiments and preparations for the journey to the Pole. He sorted out the food and equipment that would be needed. It was divided and arranged into the stores that would be needed for the trip to the Pole and those to be kept for the return trip. Scott did not need to worry about his route. He had decided to follow Shackleton's path. There were no serious obstacles blocking this route, and he knew there was a possible path leading up the Beardmore Glacier.

Amundsen had no scientific problems to worry him. He concentrated all his efforts on the dash to the Pole. Unlike Scott, he had reason to be concerned about the ground he was to travel over. Nobody had

crossed the Ice Shelf from the Bay of Whales before and no one was certain that there was another route through the mountains other than over the Beardmore Glacier. Amundsen would travel faster than Scott, but he had no idea what natural barriers he might find. The race to the Pole would be decided by geography. If Amundsen could find an easy route, he would win. If not, Scott would be the first to reach the South Pole.

Above Captain Scott in his hut, preparing for the journey to the Pole.

Far left This map shows the routes to the South Pole taken by Shackleton, Scott and Amundsen.

Below Dr. Atkinson in his small laboratory. Much of the expedition's scientific work was performed here.

Scaling the Glaciers

When the sun appeared and signaled the beginning of spring, both Scott and Amundsen began to make their final preparations. Amundsen packed his four sleds with everything he was going to need. He exercised his dogs to try to make them as fit as possible. From his group of over a hundred dogs he selected fifty-two animals as the finest and best suited for the journey. On October 19 Amundsen set out. He would soon know if his decision to find a new route south was a wise one.

Meanwhile, Scott had work to do before he could set off. The team needed to collect instruments and information that they had left west of the Ferrar Glacier. A meeting was held to decide who would return home on the *Terra Nova* and who would stay on for another winter. Several scientists, whose work had been completed, decided to go back but most of them wanted to stay. On November 1 the southern party, as it was called, set out for the South Pole.

Scott's plan was to use the two motorized sleds to carry supplies as far as possible. Everybody knew that these unreliable machines would break down – it was simply a matter of when. After the motorized sleds had been abandoned, the dogs and ponies would haul the stores and supplies as far as they could. Stores of food and fuel would be left along the route. As the sleds were emptied, they would be sent back to the base camp until just one sled and four men remained for the final journey to the South Pole.

Above *Roald Amundsen on his skis.*

Below *The Beardmore Glacier, across which Scott traveled.*

The motorized sleds traveled only a short distance before they broke down. Stores were transferred to the ten pony sleds and two dog teams and were also stacked on sleds pulled by men. The ponies did better than Scott had expected. He thought they would collapse early in the journey and had decided that they would be killed and their meat would be stored or fed to the dogs. In fact, they dragged the sleds slowly, but over a long distance. Five of the ponies managed to travel all the way across the Ice Shelf, even though a blizzard held the party up for five days. At the foot of the Beardmore Glacier they were shot, and their meat was buried for later use. The dog teams were then sent back with the empty sleds.

The twelve men set out to drag their sleds up the glacier. The Beardmore Glacier is 160 km (100 mi) long and rises nearly 3,000 m (9,842 ft) to the plateau. The climb was long and tiring. A member of the party fell through a layer of snow into a crevasse 20 m (65 ft) deep. Only his harness saved him from death. By Christmas Day they had climbed the glacier. Food supplies were left behind for the returning party, and the team enjoyed a huge dinner.

Amundsen had a quicker journey. On the Ice Shelf, his team raced along by allowing the dogs to tow the men as well as the sleds. "That was a pleasant surprise," he wrote. "We had never dreamed of driving on skis to the Pole."

Having left a few days earlier, Amundsen had avoided the blizzard that had delayed Scott. But a new problem presented itself. As the Norwegians advanced across the ice, a barrier of mountains called the Queen Maud Range came into view. It seemed to block the path to the Pole.

Then a scar was seen running through the crags. It was a glacier. Amundsen called it the Axel Heiberg Glacier. He began the climb, which was much steeper and more difficult than the glacier that was faced by Scott. Only with great difficulty did the dogs manage to scramble over the ice and snow and reach the top. It was a dangerous journey, but eventually Amundsen drove his sleds onto the plateau.

Above Day, Nelson and Lashly dragging their heavily loaded sled up the face of a glacier. Such work required much effort and tired the men greatly.

The Race South

Once they had climbed the glaciers, both teams faced an unbroken stretch of level ground all the way to the Pole. The journey of about 400 km (250 mi) was going to consist of monotonous marches across bare Antarctic landscape. But Amundsen had reached the plateau well in advance of Scott. It seemed certain that the Norwegian would win the race.

Having reached the top of the glacier, Amundsen killed twenty-four of his dogs. The meat was chopped up. Some was fed to the remaining dogs, some was cooked for the men and the rest stored for future use. The Norwegians then put the remaining dogs in harness and set off across the plateau. There were minor upsets when sleds ran into hard ridges of ice, but such events were rare. As he had done on the Ice Shelf, Amundsen traveled at a high speed and sometimes allowed the dogs to drag the men as well as the loaded sleds.

On December 7, Amundsen reached the farthest point achieved by Shackleton. To celebrate this he unfolded the Norwegian flag and attached it to one of his sleds. With his flag flying, Amundsen set out on the final 160 km (100 mi) stretch to the Pole. "The last eight days of our outward march we had sunshine all the time," he recorded. Amundsen raced on; the Pole was within his grasp.

When Scott reached the summit of the Beardmore Glacier, he had a difficult decision to make. He had to decide who to take with him to the Pole and who to send back to the base. After much thought, Scott decided to take Dr. Wilson, Petty Officer Evans, Captain Oates and "Birdie" Bowers. The final sled was packed with enough food to last five men for a month, which was enough time to reach the Pole and return to the first store of food.

Lt. Evans and two others, Lashly and Crean, were to return to the base camp with the second sled. Their return journey was a great adventure. At first all went well, but partway down the Beardmore Glacier the sled ran out of control. The three men managed to scramble on board as it sped down the slope. "The speed at one point must have reached 60 miles an hour [100 kph] and there was danger of our end being in sight." The three men realized they were racing toward a deep crevasse. The sled left the edge of the hole and flew through the air. It crashed into the ice beyond and threw the men out violently. Luckily they landed in deep snow, and neither the explorers nor the sled were badly damaged.

After this lucky escape the men drove on for several weeks, until Lt. Evans fell ill. About 320 km (200 mi) from the base camp, Evans collapsed. He begged the others to leave him there and drive on. Lashly and Crean refused because they realized that this would mean a slow death for Evans. They heaved him on the sled and pulled it onward, although they were becoming ill themselves. When they could drag the sled no farther, the men separated. Lashly stayed with Evans while Crean ran on. After a terrible journey that lasted eighteen hours, Crean staggered into the base camp. A rescue party set out and saved Lashly and Evans. As these adventures were taking place, Scott and his companions set out on their slow but steady journey to the Pole.

At the Pole

After unfolding his national flag, Amundsen raced on with his remaining dogs. Eight days later they camped just 25 km (15 mi) from the Pole. He and his men found it difficult to sleep that night. Amundsen wrote that the excitement was like he remembered "as a little boy on the night before Christmas." The next day his team drove on until, at 3 pm, they finally stood at the Pole.

Amundsen measured the position of the sun to confirm his calculations, and then tramped a 19-km (12-mi) circuit of the Pole just to make sure that he had really got there. Certain that they were at the Pole, the Norwegians planted their flag and took photographs. They set up camp and rested for three days before setting out on the return journey. Amundsen left behind him a tent, a sled, some instruments and a letter for Scott. Then, urging his dogs up to full speed, he set off for his ship, the *Fram*.

After leaving Lt. Evan's group, Scott and his companions pushed on across the snow. After twelve days they were just 40 km (25 mi) from the Pole. Until this point there had been no sign of the Norwegians. Scott hoped that Amundsen had not found a route onto the plateau and that the Pole was still unconquered. On January 16 they came across a small flag and part of a sled and saw tracks in the snow.

Above *Captain Scott and his men at the Pole. Those standing are: from left to right, Wilson, Scott and Oates, in front of them are Bowers and Evans.*

Left *When Amundsen and his men reached the South Pole, they raised the Norwegian flag.*

"All the day dreams must go," wrote Scott. They now knew that Amundsen had reached the Pole before them.

On January 18, Scott, Bowers, Wilson, Oates and Evans reached Amundsen's abandoned tent. Scott read the letter that Amundsen had left him.

"Dear Captain Scott,–As you probably are the first to reach this area after us, I will ask you kindly to forward this letter to King Haakon VII. If you can use any of the articles left in the tent, please do so. The sled left outside might be of use to you. With kind regards, I wish you a safe return.

Yours truly,

Roald Amundsen."

Scott left a note stating the date on which he had found the tent. The Union Jack was planted in the snow and the five men took a photograph of themselves. Their faces show their disappointment. Scott and his men were now faced with a trek of 1,300 km (800 mi) across the frozen landscape before they could hope to see a human face again. After a night's rest at the Pole, they set out on their homeward journey.

The Return

After leaving the Pole, Amundsen drove his dogs across the plateau. The weather remained good for him, and after only a few weeks he was at the top of the Axel Heiberg Glacier. Although he had some difficulty getting his dogs down the steep, broken surface of the ice, Amundsen reached the Ice Shelf safely. He then urged his remaining dogs to run faster and raced off across the ice.

On January 25, Amundsen reached the *Fram* after a journey of just ninety-nine days. He found that a Japanese team of scientists had also arrived in the Bay of Whales. He stopped to greet them before loading his men and equipment onto the *Fram* and sailing toward civilization. After a trouble-free voyage, he arrived in Hobart, Tasmania, and spread the news of his success around the world. He then set out to enjoy the praise of the public for his achievement.

Scott, meanwhile, was still battling his way through the snow. The first few days after leaving the Pole the five men traveled well. Knowing that the wind on the plateau generally blew away from the Pole, Scott had taken a sail with him to help pull the sled. This was now fastened on top of the sled and the team set off at great speed. The men could march quickly because they didn't need to pull their sled. A day's journey of 32 km (20 mi) was not unusual.

Then the direction of the winds, which had always been southerly, changed. The sail had to be taken down and the sled was hauled by the five men. For this, the team used special harnesses that had been designed by Scott after his earlier expedition.

Suddenly a blizzard struck. They were forced to make camp

and shelter until it was over. Scott wrote in his diary, "I don't like the look of it. Is the weather breaking up? If so God help us." When the team was able to start again, they found the traveling more and more difficult and the weather ever more cold. They were nearly always hungry. The food stores would have been enough for them if they had managed to keep up the speed of the outward march, but they were now beginning to get tired.

Their main problem was their diet. At the time of the expedition the importance of vitamins was not really known. Although Scott had sought expert medical advice about their food, the scientists had been wrong. The food they were eating lacked important vitamins and minerals. This slowed the men down and made them feel the cold more than they should have.

Despite these problems the men plodded on. Suddenly Scott and Evans vanished from sight as they fell into a hidden crevasse. Scott was unhurt, but before they could be rescued, Evans was badly dazed. They reached the food depot at the top of the Beardmore Glacier on February 7. The men were still thinking about their scientific work and they collected samples of rocks from the area before beginning the march down the glacier. Everything was going well until Evans began to stumble. He had not recovered from his fall into the crevasse. This was the first sign of approaching disaster.

Journey's End

Scott's party managed to get their sled down the glacier, but it was clear that Evans was becoming very ill. Soon after leaving the glacier, on February 16, Evans's boots became loose. He stopped to do them up while the others trudged on. When Evans did not catch up with them, Scott went back to find him. He found Evans kneeling in the snow, with his clothes undone, muttering to himself. The team made camp and tried to revive him. But it was a hopeless task and at midnight Evans finally died.

Scott, Oates, Wilson and Bowers set out again after a few hours rest to cross the Ice Shelf. There were food supplies at regular intervals on which the men could rely. All they needed to do was to travel an average of 16 km (10 mi) each day and they would reach their base safely. This was not impossible, but luck turned against the group.

Fresh blizzards had blown across the Ice Shelf since their outward journey and had covered the ice with deep snow. This made traveling difficult and, because they were so tired and weak, the men could only manage 10 km (6 mi) a day. Food was becoming scarce, as was the fuel needed to cook it. The most dangerous thing was the cold, which was now around –30° C (–22° F). Frostbite was affecting everybody. This condition reduces strength and is incredibly painful. Oates was the worst sufferer. By March 7 his feet were a mass of frostbite

Below In a heroic attempt to save his friends' lives, Captain Oates walked to his death in a blizzard.

we shall stick it out
to the end but we
are getting weaker of
course and the end
cannot be far.
It seems a pity, but
I do not think I can
write more —
R Scott

Last Entry —
For Gods Sake look
after our people

and gangrene (a disease that makes the flesh rot because the blood supply is cut off). He could no longer pull the sled and trudged along in constant pain.

By March 11 it was clear that Oates was dying. Although he was slowing them down and lowering their own chances of survival, the team refused to leave him to die in the snow. They forced him to walk on. On the morning of March 17 the party could not leave their tent because of a blizzard. Realizing that he might cause the death of his friends, Oates stood up and opened the tent door. "I am just going outside and may be some time," he said. He disappeared into the snow, walking to his death to save his companions. "It was the act of a brave man and an English gentleman," wrote Scott in his diary.

For eight more days the men struggled toward the safety of the food store known as One Ton Depot. On the evening of March 19 they pitched camp just 18 km (11 mi) from their target. That night, a fierce blizzard swept down onto the tent. Every day they made ready to start out for their journey to safety, but the blizzard never stopped. By March 29 Scott admitted to himself that they were doomed. He wrote in his diary, "We shall stick it out to the end, but we are getting weaker, of course, and the end cannot be far. It seems a pity, but I cannot write more." Then he signed his name and added, "For God's sake look after our people." Even when he was near to his own death, Scott was thinking of the other members of his team. The men lay in their tent and died.

Above left The cairn built by Atkinson and the search party to mark the last resting place of Scott and his companions.

Above right The final page of Scott's diary, containing his last words.

The Legacy of Scott

A search party set out in the spring. This group was led by the surgeon, Atkinson. On November 12, 1912, they found the tent containing the bodies of Scott, Bowers and Wilson. The search party collected their diaries, writings and records and built a huge mound of snow over their bodies. They held a burial service and erected a cross made out of skis. Atkinson and his men then began their journey back to carry the news of Scott's death to the world.

The immediate reaction to their announcement was shock that such a disaster could have happened to such a well-equipped team. Then, as details became known, this feeling was replaced by pride in the courage and achievements of the dead men. The heroic action of Captain Oates was referred to in books and magazines as perhaps the greatest act of self-sacrifice possible. The efforts of the dead men were an example to everybody. Scott himself had realized this as he lay dying. He wrote, "After all, we are setting a good example to our countrymen, if not by getting into a tight place, by facing it like men when we were there."

The scientific work of the expedition had proved vitally important to an understanding of the Antarctic. Perhaps most important of all were the rocks gathered by Scott on the Beardmore Glacier. These dated back some 200 million years and contained fossils proving that Antarctica had once been a lush, tropical country. Identical fossils in South Africa and

Below The positions of the continents 180 million years ago and today. The geological samples brought back by Scott's party forced geologists to rethink their ideas about the history of the Earth. Eventually scientists recognized that Antarctica, like other continents, had moved around the globe in the course of prehistory.

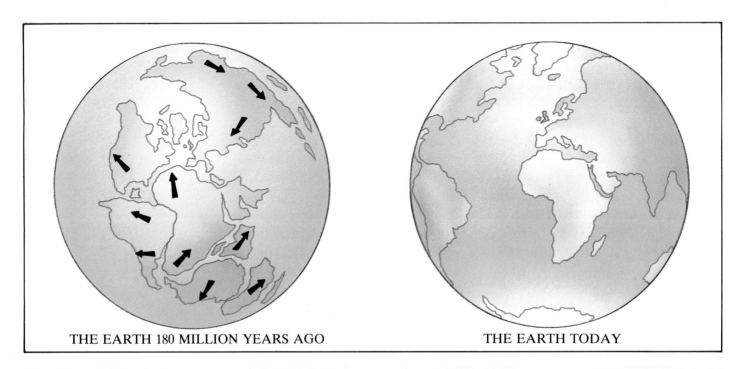

THE EARTH 180 MILLION YEARS AGO   THE EARTH TODAY

Above The sophisticated technology of today's polar explorers.

Above The team of the British Commonwealth Expedition, which crossed Antarctica in 1957.

South America showed that the three continents had once been joined together.

The scientific work and heroism of the party encouraged future explorations. In 1912 a team led by the Australian Douglas Mawson explored large new territories. Two years later Shackleton led a major expedition to the Antarctic. In 1921 he set off on yet another, although he died during the expedition. During the 1920s and 1930s, a large number of expeditions set out, some of which were equipped with airplanes.

The climax of this interest came in 1946, when Admiral Richard Byrd of the United States led 4,700 men and 13 ships to Antarctica. They mapped vast new areas and discovered mountain ranges nobody even thought existed.

In 1957 a British Commonwealth team succeeded in crossing the continent from the Weddel Sea to the Ross Ice Shelf. In 1959 an international treaty was signed that restricted activity on Antarctica to peaceful and scientific work.

Today there are 57 permanent bases on Antarctica, which are operated by scientists from 18 nations. We are learning more and more about this desolate continent. The vital importance of the region to the world's weather and ocean currents is slowly being understood. The bases are equipped with the advantages of technology. They have motorized transportation, heating systems, radio contact with the outside world and highly sensitive scientific instruments. These bases would never have been possible without the scientific work carried out by Scott and Shackleton, who risked their lives for the advancement of knowledge.

Glossary

Antarctica The continent that surrounds the South Pole.

Blizzard A fierce storm in which snow falls heavily and the wind blows strongly.

Chart To make a detailed plan or a map.

Climate The normal temperature and weather conditions of a certain country or area.

Continent A vast area of land. There are seven continents in the world.

Crevasse A deep crack in snow and ice, often hidden by a thin crust. This surface breaks when someone walks on it, and many explorers have died after falling into a crevasse.

Expedition A journey made for a special reason, such as to explore an unknown area.

Experiment A test made by a scientist. The results of these tests are used to find out something previously unknown.

Geographer Someone who studies the Earth, including its land formations, plants, climates and peoples.

Geologist Someone who studies rocks and land formations.

Glacier A mass of ice that moves slowly down a valley or mountain. It looks rather like a frozen river.

Iceberg A huge lump of ice that floats in the sea. Icebergs usually form in polar regions when a glacier breaks up.

Ice floe A large, flat sheet of ice that forms a crust on the sea in very cold areas. An ice floe looks like the ice that forms on a pond during the winter.

Leave The time allowed members of the armed forces away from their duties, when they can do as they like.

Mechanized transportation Means of transportation that are powered by motors.

Meteorologist Someone who studies the climate and the weather.

Minerals Substances that are found in many foods and are needed for good health.

Naturalist A scientist who studies the world of nature.

Observatory A special building with powerful telescopes for observing the stars and planets.

Plateau An area of high-lying flat land, often surrounded by mountains.

Siberian To do with Siberia, which is a huge and very cold region of the USSR.

South Pole The southernmost point on the Earth's axis. The North Pole is the Earth's northernmost point.

Specimen Something that is collected and then preserved as an example to be studied away from its natural habitat.

Sponsor An individual or group that helps someone or something, often by giving money.

Sub-zero A phrase that is used to describe temperatures that are below freezing point (0° C, 32° F).

Theories Ideas, not always based on known facts, that are used to explain complicated problems.

Vitamins Substances found in food and needed for good health. A lack of vitamins can cause many illnesses.

Finding Out More

Antarctica has been split into territories that are administered by different governments. Most of these territories contain permanent bases in which scientists can work throughout the year. You can find out about the work of these scientists by contacting the following addresses:

U.S. Antarctic Research Program
Division of Polar Programs
National Science Foundation
1800 G Street, NW
Washington, DC 20550
Phone: 202–357–7817

Dr. Charles Bentley
Geophysical and Polar Research Center
Dept. of Geology and Geophysics
University of Wisconsin
Madison, Wisconsin 53706

The British Antarctic Survey
High Cross
Maddingley Road
Cambridge
CB3 0ET

The Publicity Officer
Antarctic Division
Commonwealth Government of Australia
Channel Highway
Kingston, Tasmania 7050

The Antarctic Manager
The Department of Science and Industrial
    Resources
Commonwealth Government of New Zealand
PO Box 1578
Wellington

Books to Read

Antarctica by Gardner Soule
    (Franklin Watts, 1985)
The Arctic and Antarctic by Cass R. Sandak
    (Franklin Watts, 1987)
A Closer Look at Arctic Lands by Jill Hughes
    (Gloucester Press, 1987)
Eskimos by Jill Hughes
    (Gloucester Press, 1984)
Living in Polar Regions by Theodore A. Rees
    Cheney (Franklin Watts, 1987)

Picture Acknowledgments

The publishers would like to thank the following for allowing their illustrations to be reproduced in this book:

The Mansell Collection 18 (top); Popperfoto 4, 5 (top), 6 (top), 7 (bottom), 8, 10 (three cameo portraits), 11 (three cameo portraits), 23, 27 (left); The Royal Geographical Society 5 (bottom), 10, 11 (top left), 13 (top and bottom), 17 (top and bottom), 18 (bottom), 19 (top), 29 (right); Topham Picture Library *frontispiece*, 6 (bottom), 15, 20, 27 (right), 29 (left); Wayland Picture Library 7 (top). The cover artwork and all maps and diagrams are by Peter Bull Art Studio.

Index